# Tell Me About the Hard Part

## FIVE STEPS to HELP BUSINESSES FACE, SOLVE & PREVENT PROBLEMS

OPEN
FOR
BUSINESS

## by SHAVON J. SMITH, Esq.

Published by
ELOHAI International Publishing & Media
P.O. Box 1883
Cypress, Texas 77410
www.elohaiintl.com

Author Contact
The SJS Law Firm, PLLC
1775 I Street NW Suite 1150
Washington, D.C. 20006
info@thesjslawfirm.com
www.TheSJSLawFirm.com

ISBN: 978-1-953535-71-9

Printed in the United States of America

# Table of Contents

# Acknowledgements

This book was a God idea… At a conference in 2018 the idea dropped in my spirit very suddenly. While I was not obedient in finishing my assignment quickly, I thank God for trusting me with this idea.

To my clients who trust me with their businesses, I do not take it lightly and have learned so much from each of you. I am blessed to wake up and work in a business I created with people I like and respect tremendously.

To each of my friends who over the years have served as a council of advisors for my business. Thank you to Christopher Issacs, Robin Terry, Ulani Prater Gulestone, Aja Sae Kung (who referred my first client to me!) Charles Anamelechi, Renette Jackson, and Erik Williams—for taking my calls and lending your ear. Especially Attorney William C. McCaskill whose sage advice has been instrumental in my journey.

To the team at ELOHAI International Publishing & Media for their patience and detailed work, and the CEO, Natasha Brown Watson, who I happened to meet years ago at the same conference where this idea was birthed.

To all of my friends and my entire family, sister, niece, aunts, uncles, and cousins who have supported me and prayed for me in my journey as an attorney and business owner.

Finally, to my mother and father (God rest his soul). On December 25, 2002 my parents presented me a Bible with the following inscription: "When things go wrong, don't go with them. Go to the Word for the peace that passes all understanding. Trust God." I have used this as my life's guiding principle…you should too.

# Foreword

*"Running away from your problems is a race you'll never win."*

When Shavon and I first met circa 2007, I wish she had given me *Tell Me About the Hard Part*, it would have probably prevented me from making some costly mistakes. I was in my early twenties when I decided to make a profession out of being an entrepreneur, and since then, I've helped launch companies in a wide range of industries, such as healthcare, government contracting, internet technology, and agriculture. For almost two decades, Shavon has been not just a personal friend, but also a valued advisor and attorney.

My first and enduring impression of Shavon is that of a poker-faced lawyer from "The D". We both have ties to our mutual alma mater Howard University, and when we met on the D.C. social scene, we quickly discovered we had mutual friends. I learned very early that Shavon, like an onion, has many layers: she is practical, stoic, very bright, hard-working, family-oriented, caring, humble, and has do-the-right-thing principles rooted firmly in her Midwest roots.

I've gotten to know Shavon through our mutual passion for cuisine, travel, and entrepreneurship. She has a great palate, and her flawless etiquette will never have her come to a dinner party empty handed. We have enjoyed many meals together in cities such as Amsterdam, Dubai, Durban, Lisbon, and our beloved Washington, D.C., where we've discussed a wide range of life and business topics.

As I mentioned at the outset, I really wish I had read *Tell Me About the Hard Part* when I was first starting out, but even as a seasoned business owner, I found it to be quite helpful in laying the groundwork for future success. All business owners, no matter what stage their company is in, can use the book's five pillars as a guide to constructing a solid foundation for their enterprise.

The first section of the book that explores the Face IT step is my favorite since it is where I have learned the most as a business owner and where I believe most firms, especially startups and small enterprises, suffer. (1) Systems and processes, (2) spending time working on the business, (3) establishing key indicators, (4) listening to your customers, (5) embracing difficult conversations, and (6) creating an emotional support system. Detailed and applicable; I can confidently state that each and every one of these components was present in every thriving enterprise I've ever run or witnessed.

*Tell Me About the Hard Part* focuses on five steps that businesses can take to address, solve, and prevent problems in their operations. Shavon expertly draws a connection between business and problem solving, and then organizes the phases of problem solving into a framework for achieving success.

As a lawyer in Washington, D.C., Shavon has a unique and broad viewpoint because of her experiences and exposure with various small business owners. Whether running an HVAC company, as the book's example does, or a government contracting firm, international commerce corporation, cannabis shop, or any other business, she is seasoned.

In this way, *Tell Me About the Hard Part* is useful because it provides a road map that can be followed by entrepreneurs at any level and in any field to create a more prosperous and sustainable enterprise.

Christopher T. Issacs
Entrepreneur

# Preface

*"If wisdom is an old man, humbleness is his younger self."*
—Attorney William C. McCaskill

**Proverbs 1:1–9 (KJV) – Wisdom's Beginnings**

The proverbs of Solomon the son of David, king of Israel; To know wisdom and instruction; to perceive the words of understanding; To receive the instruction of wisdom, justice, and judgment, and equity; To give subtilty to the simple, to the young man knowledge and discretion; A wise man will hear, and will increase learning; and a man of understanding shall attain unto wise counsels; To understand a proverb, and the interpretation; the words of the wise, and their dark sayings; The fear of the LORD is the beginning of knowledge but fools despise wisdom and instruction; My son, hear the instruction of thy father, and forsake not the law of thy mother; For they shall be an ornament of grace unto thy head, and chains about thy neck.

I have a podcast entitled *Tell Me About the Hard Part*, where I interview business owners at various stages of business. My final question to the interviewees on each episode is always, *"Tell Me About the Hard Part* of running your business." The answers have a wide range, for sure, but generally involve hiring, firing, and locating worthwhile collaborations (people); access to credit and having cash to cover immediate expenses, such as payroll (money); being visible and reaching enough of their target market (marketing and branding); and staying encouraged for the journey (mindset), to name a few. These were all the things that were hinderances and stood in the way of fully accomplishing why they went into business in the first place and threatened to derail their mission.

For many of the business owners I have had the privilege of speaking with, either on my podcast or in my law practice, the overwhelming reasons they went into business were either they saw a problem no one was solving (or not solving well) and knew they could or they simply wanted to help people in some form or fashion, whether by making their lives easier, employing them, or bringing them a solution. And then here come these "hard parts." However, when you figure out a consistent method to move past these things, people, and circumstances that attempt to derail you, you will be a more successful business owner and achieve your mission as a business owner.

In life as in business (aren't they really one and the same?), problems are there to help us learn, grow, improve, and take stock. Webster defines a "problem" as "a source of perplexity, distress, or vexation" but also as "a question raised for inquiry, consideration, or solution." The definition instructs us that problems force us to ask questions, and when put in proper perspective, they can be our guidepost to the business and life we desire.

So although they vex us, some problems can serve as signs that your business is growing. How? If everything was perfect, that would mean you have it all figured out and that you and your business are on autopilot. You cannot grow while on autopilot; there's nothing new to learn there. You have to be out of your comfort zone, and problems and crises do that. The whole purpose of this book is to teach you concrete steps to work past your business problems and use them as catalysts and guideposts to actually improve your business.

I have had the pleasure of working with owners of small and medium-sized businesses since 2014, solving both their legal and non-legal problems. I've worked with hundreds of businesses and solved even more problems. The steps described in this book have long been my mental checklist for helping clients navigate the thorniest of issues.

# Introduction

I recently had a client complain about all of the problems she had been facing in her business. Every week there seemed to be a new nuisance or what felt like a catastrophic, business-ending issue. Some events could derail her operations, and some were just enough to distract her—unexpected bills or a less than happy customer or employee. I assured her that problems were simply part of doing business. While you should engage in consistent business and life planning, you should anticipate that most days or quarters are unlikely to follow your well-drafted script. Think of the last time you had a week or even day go exactly as planned. I'm not talking about a day when you planned to binge watch Netflix (that always seems to go swimmingly) but a day that involved people or leaving the house—or your bedroom even. Not to say you will not get close, but when have you reached perfection? We are people and, by nature, flawed and far from free of fault or defect. By correlation then, the businesses and projects we create will not be free of fault or defect either.

There are some seasoned entrepreneurs who are ecstatic about problems, who embrace our collective human state as lacking perfection. They see opportunity in our flaws because these individuals know there is always room for improvement, always a better way, always innovation afoot. They also know that solving problems, even those things that you did not know were problems, is how billionaires are birthed. (Think Amazon or Facebook. Did you even know you needed groceries and batteries delivered in an hour or even care what your third grade teacher was up to?) They expect challenges and also know that their greatest triumphs are on the other side of obstacles. They also know that finding a way to navigate business obstacles is how one moves closer to success.

I recently admitted there were some aspects of my life that I did not like—so many issues I felt like I was dealing with. A friend helped me realize that meant I recognized there were things that made me uncomfortable, and if I was uncomfortable enough, I would make changes. Problems force us to make changes—either willingly or by force.

So even in these few short paragraphs, I hope you have embraced that whatever business problem you may be facing is probably not that bad and could signal greater times ahead if you successfully navigate through it. But now what? Now that you're calm about it (hopefully!), how do you work through it? Who do you talk to? Every problem is unique. There is no magic pill, and the bigger the problem, the more energy it may take to solve. However, there is a formula you can implement to start seeing straight and navigating to the other side:

I.　Face It
II.　Diagnose It
III.　Quantify It
IV.　Treat It
V.　Prevent It

a. **Face it:** The first step in solving any problem is to recognize you have a problem! This is twofold: 1) not ignoring what is right in front of you and 2) spending time to finetune your business so you can uncover weak spots before they morph into full-blown problems.

b. **Diagnose it:** Define the problem. Here, we are getting to what the real issue is (i.e., what type of problem do you have?). The problems are categorized into types since knowing the type of problem you are facing will lead to a deeper analysis of what's really going on.

c. **Quantify it:** What is this problem worth? How much will this cost me now, how much will it cost me later, and how much will it cost me if I never even address it—what will I lose? Will the problem bankrupt me, or is it just a nuisance? Who and how much do I have to pay to fix or even alleviate the problem?

d. **Treat it:** Ways to treat the actual problem will come from a range of options—hire, fire, cash flow, marketing, branding—but also a range of professionals specifically trained for the problem at hand.

e. **Prevent it:** What's the point of solving it if you're just going to get right back into the same mess? This section will hearken back to Chapter 1 and answers the following questions: What systems can you have in place to continuously monitor? What do you need to permanently change, and what pieces are missing to sustain your business through less than desirable conditions? Prevention is like the wise man or woman who builds their house on a rock; they know treacherous conditions are bound to come in life and that one has to prepare.

First, we will tackle step one—"face it"—where we will discuss ways to help you see that you have problems that need to be addressed. Next, we will "diagnose it" and start to categorize the types of problems you may face. Thirdly, "quantify it" is where we discuss how costly or crucial the problem is. Thereafter, in "treat it," we will dive into the types of solutions that may be needed for your problems. Finally, we will "prevent it," and you will learn steps to move toward averting future possible problems. Throughout the book, you'll get to know James "Jim" Monroe, the owner of Monroe HVAC (not a real person or company). Jim and his issues are a compilation of my clients over the years. Working through Jim's issue will be a way for you to see the process in action.

I hope that in reading this book, eventually these steps will become second nature to you, as they are to me—so much so that you will consistently run through the list as you are managing all aspects of your business or turn back to each chapter as needed over time.

Crisis has a way of getting us to focus. Jesus never showed up to perform a miracle unless a miracle was needed. I hope in reading this book, you will adapt the following mindset:

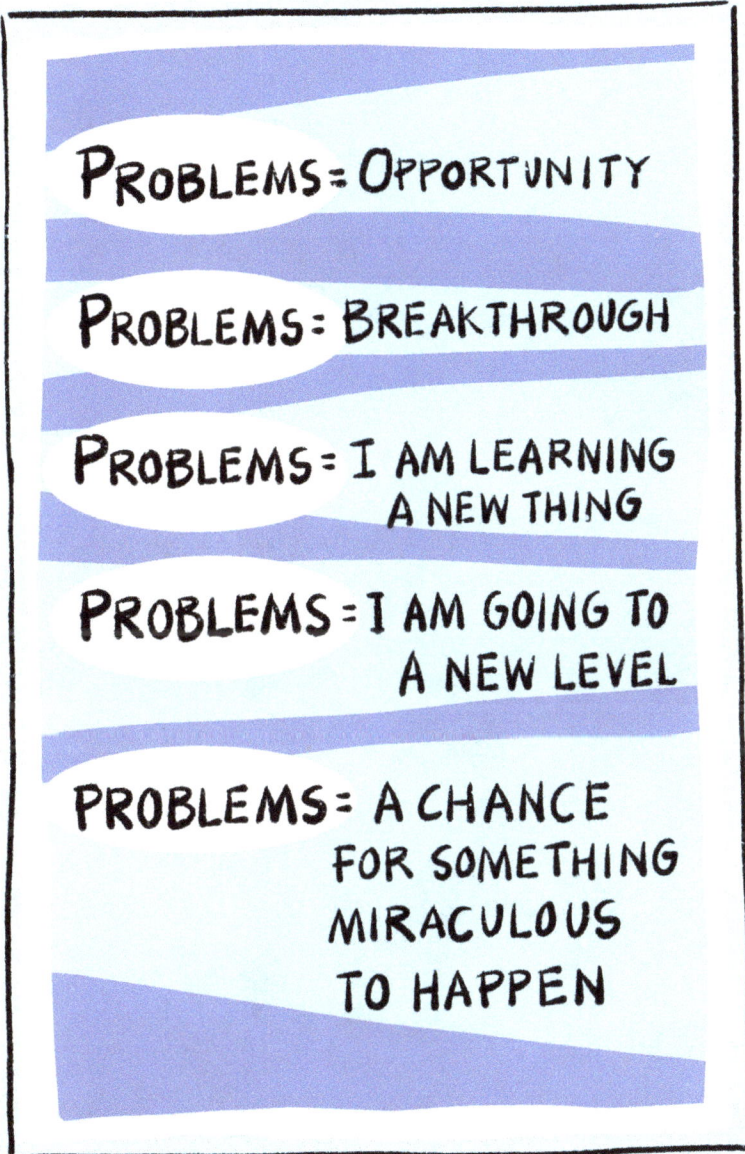

PROBLEMS = OPPORTUNITY

PROBLEMS = BREAKTHROUGH

PROBLEMS = I AM LEARNING A NEW THING

PROBLEMS = I AM GOING TO A NEW LEVEL

PROBLEMS = A CHANCE FOR SOMETHING MIRACULOUS TO HAPPEN

# Chapter 1

*Not everything that is faced can be changed,*
*but nothing can be changed unless it's faced.*

## FACE IT

You cannot even begin to solve a problem that you will not acknowledge. Even still, the hardest part for most business owners is
to—you guessed it—face that they have a problem. Just moments
ago, I had a conversation with a business owner who is regulated
by a state agency in his industry. He had a problem that he knew
existed and knew had to be dealt with or risk dire consequences,
but he continued to ignore multiple communications from the
state agency on the issue because he simply did not want to deal
with it. So to be clear, he knew it had to be faced; he just put off
doing so for as long as possible. Perhaps he thought it would go
away, but rarely, if ever, does a problem just "go away." In fact,
he *knew* it wouldn't disappear, but sometimes the emotional toll
of diving into a particular issue is too much to bear. Also, there
are other things to be done that always seem more pressing and
important. Or you think if you focus on making money and building, somehow the problem will minimize itself.

The calls I received in my law practice from clients who waited
until they were sued (although they knew there was a simmering

dispute months ago) or sat on a problem until it completely blew up is no small number. Countless business owners wait until the last day before an answer to a complaint is due or even after a judgment is entered to contact an attorney. And a lawsuit is a *clear* business problem. My personal favorite is when business partners face strife with one another. These issues are usually slow brewing, and one fatal day it all blows up with revoked access to email and bank accounts for one partner.

Ignoring a problem generally means it grows and will cost you more to fix once you finally face it. It can't get better until you acknowledge it. As a business owner, you've made a life by doing hard things. In some instances, it's as easy as acknowledging the letter or angry email, but as your operation grows and your systems and processes do not keep up, it may not be that simple.

Here are six steps you should take to help you recognize and face your business problems:

(1) Create systems.
(2) Spend time working on the business.
(3) Establish key indicators.
(4) Listen to your customers.
(5) Embrace difficult conversations.
(6) Create an emotional support system.

**Create processes and systems.**
The earth runs on a system. Everything has its place, everything in order. Even your body and its various parts is a well-tuned

system designed to work together. Doctors know something is off if one part starts working a little differently than usual. For instance, experiencing more fatigue than normal can be an indicator that something is wrong. Your business also needs a "system"—a way it runs that makes it easy to detect any defect.

The most successful business owners I know understand that systems and processes are key to their business success. They treat their business, whether a product, service, or mix of the two, as a widget where they go from raw material to getting paid each and every time without fail (i.e., consistency). In short, a business process is a set of related, structured activities and steps performed by the people or equipment in an organization in order to achieve the basic organizational goal. A process is how the sausage is made; it's what the consumer or end user may not see. A crucial step in creating a system is understanding your company culture or values. Your processes or lack thereof are likely a reflection of your company values or your own personal values. If you believe in autonomy of your staff and a flat organization (lacking in layers), each process may not involve multiple layers or people. While one could copy and paste what someone else is doing, that simply may not work for what you are building.

Even if you do not have formal systems or processes, you do have a way you do things specific to your business, whether it's documented or not. So how do you create your business system? After thinking about your values (what's truly important to you in your business that you want to track), you'll want to write down how you do everything in your business: 1) how you onboard a client, 2) how you onboard employees, and 3) how you send invoices and collect payment. There's a way each of those things are done—that's a process. But what we're getting at here is intentionality. How can you take that and be intentional about documenting, improving, and delegating the steps as needed? What you're doing may be great; it just may not be intentional. Or it may be horrible and haphazard. You won't know if your process works until you sit and work through what you are actually doing for each component of the business and how effective it is.

Business schools spend entire semesters talking about business process. Fortune 500 companies pay consultants $1,000 an hour or more to figure out kinks in their process and develop better ones. Perhaps you have the budget for this, or you can look to these principles for process improvement. But for many small businesses that are running lean operations, a much simpler approach and methodology is warranted, especially in the beginning. There is no one-size-fits-all approach to building systems and processes in your business, but they should be simple so that everyone on the team can execute them, be standardized, and have a method for continuous review/improvement of the process.

# PRE-ONBOARDING CHECKLIST

## BE PREPARED FOR THE NEW HIRE

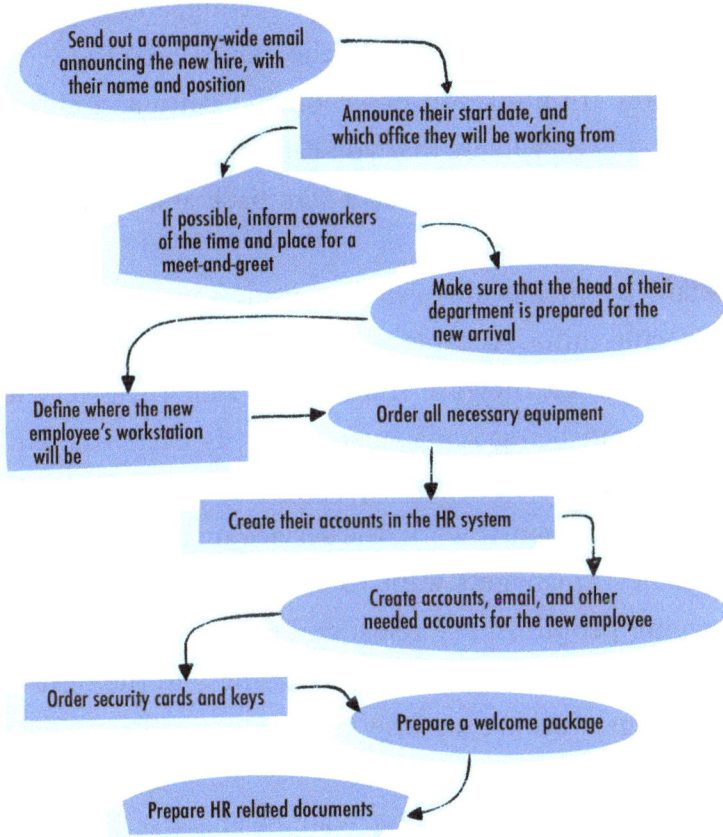

Send out a company-wide email announcing the new hire, with their name and position

Announce their start date, and which office they will be working from

If possible, inform coworkers of the time and place for a meet-and-greet

Make sure that the head of their department is prepared for the new arrival

Define where the new employee's workstation will be

Order all necessary equipment

Create their accounts in the HR system

Create accounts, email, and other needed accounts for the new employee

Order security cards and keys

Prepare a welcome package

Prepare HR related documents

### *Spend Time Working on the Business*

Yes, I know; you hear it all the time: Work on the business not just in the business. You spend so much time focused on your clients, customers, day-to-day operations, and employees that you rarely have time for big-picture thinking. Working on your business is about developing growth strategies through activities such as strategic planning, goal setting, and finetuning processes and automation. You are the genius behind the business. When you are hunkered down on the daily and entrapped in minutia, it is very likely that you can "miss it." Working on your business requires you to take a step back and take a fifty thousand foot view.

Many people decide to start a business because they are good at a specific thing. As explained in the popular *E-Myth* series by Michael Gerber, they are technicians, which is a very different skill set from being a manager, which is even still a different skill set from being an entrepreneur. In short, technicians are focused on the actual work, the service or product produced by the business; managers want to ensure optimal results through leveraging people and systems; and the entrepreneur is focused on the big picture and taking the business to the next level. I'd submit that working on the business straddles manager and entrepreneur.

Gerber advocates treating your business as if you will ultimately franchise it. In addition to the trademark or tradename, a franchise is just a series of systems: the way a particular function is done every single time. This is useful because it is easier to spot a faulty cog in a wheel when you know exactly how that wheel is supposed to work every time.

Let's look at an example: Disney theme parks. You may not have been there, but you absolutely know about them and have seen countless images of the Magic Kingdom. So what is the day to day at a Disney theme park? Getting guests in, thrilling them, feeding them, and getting them to spend money. But Disney has spent significant time creating a system to provide guests with a consistently thrilling experience. As such, Disney spends significant time collecting data on guests to make sure the system is working as designed. All of this working on Disney gives it the opportunity to design the guest experience and solutions for any possible looming issues.

You may not be a Disney theme park, but big-picture thinking and working on the business gives any business owner an opportunity to look at their systems and processes (or lack thereof) and examine the leaks in the boat that will lead to potential problems.

Joining accelerator programs, coaching, incubators, or masterminds is a great way to spend time on the business because you make a commitment to others to show up at a specific time. There, you are compelled by facilitators and peers to talk about your business in a macro way and identify challenges and opportunities for growth. Business programs will typically spend time on everything from effectively growing your team and marketing to necessary innovations and market expansion opportunities. For others that are not prone to join programs, it may just be carving out the time. Some business owners have a system (hey, there's that word again!) whereby they delegate certain activities to certain days, for instance, Mondays, marketing; Tuesdays, administrative work; Wednesdays, client meetings; Thursdays, employee meetings; Fridays, finances and strategic planning. At least two times a year, I will book a hotel room two-plus hours away to get a change of scenery and spend time working on my law practice. I am often able to work though ways to tackle challenges, goal set, track my progress for the year, and simply visualize how I want the business to look and feel.

### Establish Key Indicators

When working on the business and creating systems, the next leg in the race is to establish key performance indicators (KPIs) that are specific to your business. Disney tracks a lot of KPIs to measure success and improve operations, for instance, profit per guest, how busy the park gets on a particular day, and what the most popular attractions on Saturdays in the summer for families from the East Coast with kids are…; Disney gets into the minutia. It's unlikely you need to go that deep to start, but you do need to get specific on the data that matters to your business.

Simply put, KPIs are measurable values used by an entity as a way to keep track of and determine progress on a specific business objective. KPIs should be specific to your organization and departments within your organization but can include how many sales calls are made each month, revenue per customer, cost per lead, number of contracts signed, dollar value per contract, gross profit margin, time to convert a lead to a customer, and number of new leads each month. A good rule of thumb is to keep and monitor these measurements monthly or, at a minimum, quarterly. The frequency will depend on the actual KPI. Any drastic or even minor change in these figures could potentially trigger cause for concern and should send you and your team into investigative mode to determine if more is at play than a minor fluctuation. An increase in cost per lead could signal an increase in marketing costs that you should have a strategy for, or a decrease in the number of sales calls could be the result of poorly performing staff, which could be the result of and lead to a host of problems.

If you've delegated certain areas of your business to staff, that's great. You have a set of eyes dedicated to an area of potential problems. Be sure to train your staff to raise issues up the flagpole. Obviously you do not want every problem on your desk, but as you read the rest of this book, you will learn how to train your employees on which problems deserve your attention.

A good way to both work on your business and establish KPIs is to conduct a SWOT analysis. SWOT stands for **S**trengths, **W**eaknesses, **O**pportunities, and **T**hreats. The SWOT analysis is both an internal and external analysis of a company's competitive position. You can do a SWOT analysis for the business overall but also for specific product or service lines you are considering adding or cutting. While a SWOT analysis can be conducted as a solo project, you will likely attain a more thorough analysis when you incorporate your team members. Here's a SWOT analysis I conducted for my law firm a few years ago:

## STRENGTHS

Woman

Black

Flexible approach

Individual one-on-one approach with clients

Trusted advisor

## WEAKNESSES

Inefficient use of technology

Inefficient use of data and reporting

Funding/Financial resources

Small team

Poor visibility

**S W**
**O T**

## OPPORTUNITIES

Research on creating client centered experience that I can leverage

Data on avatar

Economic challenges and pandemic can increase demand for certain legal services

Global demand for individual with experience working with small enterprises

Global interest in small business

## THREATS

Creating technology that may decrease demand
for legal sevices from attorneys

Competition from other attorneys with incresed
use of technology

Economic challenges may damper demand
for certain legal services

Larger law firms looking to serve smaller enterprises

Increased regulation

### *Listen to Your Customers*

Folks have no problem telling you where you have failed or are about to. Sometimes these messages are broadcast for the world to see on social media. Even if that's not the case for your business, it is not difficult to develop a process, determine what your client experience is, and issue spot from there. Surveys are a free and easy way to obtain information from your customers that can help you spot trends related to problems you may face. But do not shy away from talking directly to your clients. If you have a retail-based business, it's easy to strike up a conversation with customers. If you have a product-based business, eliciting feedback can be a part of the order fulfillment process. For other industries, you can create regular points in the year where you check in with customers via telephone or a site visit. This information will be invaluable to finding even hairline cracks that could show up as problems down the line. As a bonus, interviewing your customers is also a great way to dig deeper into their fears, desires, and habits—all important aspects for knowing who your ideal client is and, more importantly, exactly how you can reach more of them through your marketing strategy. Simply checking in with clients and asking, "What are your biggest pain points? Even if they are not in our wheelhouse, we may know of resources to assist," can help you obtain valuable information.

### *Have the Difficult Conversations*

Learning to have difficult conversations and really embracing them is one of the cornerstones of being a business owner. In fact, the crux of facing your problems will very likely entail the need to have difficult conversations, either with yourself, business partners, employees, or customers, to name a few. Like a doctor diagnosing an illness, you have to ask uncomfortable, sometimes embarrassing, questions to fully understand the problem.

No one signs up for difficult conversations, but if you must have one—or several—here are a few tips: (1) Understand what you hope to gain and why you're having the conversation. (2) You may need to practice exactly what you are going to say, either out loud or by writing it down. (3) I want to say control your emotions, but then you'd be a robot, wouldn't you? So do not turn them off but be mindful of them and how extreme pendulums of emotion may cloud the point you are trying to make and issue you are attempting to solve. (4) With that being said, come armed with facts and quantifiable information. Logically articulate the data points that lead to your conclusion. You are less likely to be swayed by your emotions or theirs when you keep the conversation fact based. (5) Be open. Do not be so hard and fast in your position that you ignore factors that may alter your conclusion and ultimately lead to a better outcome. (6) Lead with grace and a willingness to give the benefit of the doubt. Think the highest thought about the situation and the person.

The most obvious type of difficult conversation for a business owner may be facing an issue with an underperforming employee. No business owner takes lightly that employees and their families depend on them. Employers, especially small employers, rarely want to let a person go (unless their actions are egregious). Conversations with creditors, landlords, and banks are equally hard when you know you can't make payments that month or your creditor, landlord, or lender is taking draconian actions (which they are prone to do) and you feel like you do not have many cards to play or the deep pockets to withstand their actions.

I, however, proffer that the most difficult conversations take place between business partners. Out of all the examples listed, you likely find your duty highest to your business partner, especially one that you started in the trenches with from ground zero in the business. Anyone with a business partner knows that it is much like a marriage, creating a dynamic where things can get tense quickly or brew quietly and destructively for years. Self-aware business owners realize very early (hopefully before they go into business) that they and their business partner have very different values and approaches to business. This may not in itself be a problem, but it sure can be if not managed and faced. Imagine being married and your husband or wife thinks it is okay to be massively in debt and you've never carried a credit card balance greater than thirty days. Sure, maybe you can survive that for a few years, but surely life will happen and this clear difference in values will shift into a clear problem, a clear disagreement, clear strife, and undoubted resentment.

I would be remiss if I didn't take time to discuss the emotional toll of being an entrepreneur. Often, failing to "face it" or do the hard work in your business is due to the emotional pressure, anxiety, or depression you could be experiencing. Entrepreneurs have reported higher rates of depression (30%), ADHD (29%), substance use conditions (12%), and bipolar diagnosis (11%) than non-entre-preneurs.[1] In one study, entrepreneurs reported experiencing high-er levels of stress than a comparable group of non-entrepreneurs.[2] Although the differences are not large, entrepreneurs are slightly more likely than other workers to report experiencing stress and worry.[3] In addition to those figures, I can personally attest to how isolating and lonely working for yourself can be. When you work for yourself, you may not have the built-in support system that can come when you are employed in the traditional sense. You cannot always turn to coworkers that empathize. These factors may result in making it difficult to face the problems in your business. For in-stance, having difficult conversations can be emotional work. Or perhaps it's hard to take criticism from customers because they feel like personal attacks. Not having a support system can make diffi-cult conversation and criticism even more difficult.

Creating an emotional support system (therapist, friends, prayer, exercise, diet) to support a healthy emotional state should be an important foundation in your business. You want to make sure you are making sound decisions based on facts, not on your unhealthy emotions that you have not tempered with your emotional support

---

1. Michael A. Freeman, M.D., Sheri L. Johnson, Ph.D., Paige J. Staudenmaier, and Mackenzie R. Zisser, "Are Entrepreneurs 'Touched with Fire'? (*pre-publication manu-script*)", (2015): https://michaelafreemanmd.com/.

2. Melissa S. Cardon and Pankaj C. Patel, "Is Stress Worth it? Stress-related Health and Wealth Trade-offs for Entrepreneurs," *Applied Psychology* 64, (2013).

3. Dan Witters, Sangeeta Agrawal, and Alyssa Davis, "Entrepreneurship Comes With Stress, But Also Optimism," Gallup, last modified December 7, 2012, https://news.gallup.com/poll/159131/entrepreneurship-comes-stress-optimism.aspx.

system. Some negative emotions that can be detrimental to you facing and solving your business problems are anger, anxiety, frustration, fear, loneliness, being overwhelmed, sadness, or depression.

But how did we even get here, where it's a challenge to even take the first step in solving your business woes? Why do business owners, or really people in general, have a difficult time facing problems? There is no one answer here, but I surmise that most people really just want to be liked; they care what others think (which is not inherently bad) and do not want to be seen as "mean" or "bad." Also, if your problem includes constant calls from creditors or bill collectors, you may internalize that as failure. (It is not.) Not to mention the emotional aspect of working through business issues. You begin to internalize as if you did something wrong as opposed to "something needs to be fixed in my business." You are not your business; you are you. Facing a problem, if you're doing it right, forces a great deal of self-awareness that many can't dig into, especially on their own.

## Your Next Steps

1   Identify and track at least three KPIs for each area of your business: (a) finance, (b) marketing, (c) customer service, and (d) employees/team.
2.  Conduct a SWOT analysis.
3.  Identify or develop an emotional support system.

## "Facing It" in Action

Meet business owner James Monroe; everyone calls him Jim. At thirty-two, and after working for a large regional HVAC, plumbing, and electrical company for over a decade, Jim decided to branch out on his own and start an HVAC company: Monroe Heating and Air Conditioning. Jim and his wife also had their first baby the year prior to starting the business. (They now have three boys.) He was seeking greater flexibility, control over his time, and more money to support his growing family. Jim felt like he could provide a better customer service experience and a better working environment for his technicians as well as make more money in the long run if he started his own business. Jim decided he would focus his company on HVAC instead of splitting the energy toward plumbing and electrical, which were not areas where he personally had expertise.

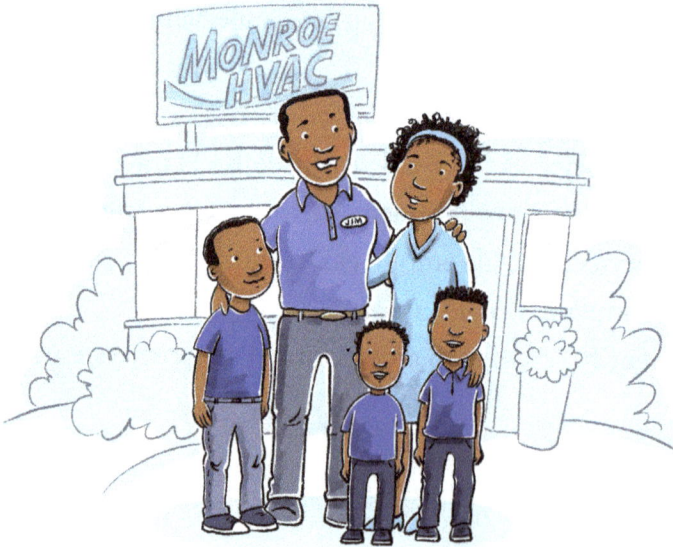

Monroe HVAC, on the cusp of their ten-year anniversary, is now thriving. They have four locations across the state, and Jim is seriously considering franchising the business. He grew from a one-man show (just him and his wife helping with the books and setting appointments) to employing seventy-five HVAC technicians and ten support staffers. Occasionally, to handle the overflow, Jim will outsource to another HVAC company. It's owned by a friend, and they have a pretty loose contract they drafted together (before Jim retained legal counsel). It's very sporadic, but when Monroe HVAC is slammed, this resource is invaluable.

He has commercials on TV—not just daytime TV but those expensive primetime slots too! It's not uncommon to hear his commercial daily or see a bus stop with his ads. From a competitor's standpoint, if you were doing your SWOT analysis, Jim would be a threat. Over the years, Jim, who had no formal business training when he started Monroe HVAC, has taken several business courses with local SBA business centers as well as online courses. He has since developed the practice of spending time looking at the business by developing and—at least monthly, sometimes weekly—looking at his KPIs. And because he is considering expansion, he has developed several SWOT analyses comparing Monroe HVAC to current and potential competitors if he decides to expand to new markets.

Internally, things are certainly not imploding, and the company is incredibly profitable. But Jim is starting to notice trends... little foxes if you will. He feels like they are not scheduling enough appointments each day, and yet all of his techs, at some point in the month, are working overtime. The overtime is further perplexing because Jim has an elaborate scheduling system that should guarantee each tech works no more than eight hours per day. It caused him to scale back on the number of appointments each tech has as the consistent overtime was affecting profitability. Now, at this point, Jim could just shrug and say, yes, this is a problem but not a *problem problem*. The business is indeed profitable (profits exceed expenses, and Jim and his staff all earn a nice salary), and Monroe HVAC generally receives good reviews—although customers often complain about techs showing up after the scheduled timeframe. These concerns were not necessarily fatal, and while Jim has experienced the typical stress that can come with entrepreneurship, these are not causing great stress and sleepless nights. However, over the years of growing his business, Jim has become an astute businessman and really a student of entrepreneurship and business ownership. So he stops and says, "There's a slight pain here that could get worse. Let me dig a bit deeper."

What's interesting here is that the issue is manifesting itself in several different ways (much like how a broken bone isn't just broken but causes redness, swelling, etc.). Here it is (1) techs working longer hours than budgeted, (2) still not getting enough appointments scheduled each day, and (3) customers starting to complain about wait times. So we have financial projections being affected with increased expense costs, human resources issues, and possible client retention concerns.

The first thing Jim casually notices is the number of appointments completed in a day. Since Jim was tracking his KPIs and had identified the number of appointments in a day as a key KPI, he is able to instantly identify an issue. Because he is still in the black, it's easy to let the early KPIs slip and think they will self-correct. It's even easier if you aren't tracking it. Next, he hones in on the customer feedback. We are not sure from our example if Monroe HVAC has a formal customer feedback process, but his customers are getting word to him, probably via Yelp or Twitter, which is my favorite way to complain! In this scenario, Jim could go a step further and have conversations with his service techs to find out why his assumptions about the number of clients they can see in an eight-hour day is so woefully off.

Jim has just taken the first step in the process and has begun to "face it." He is able to do this because he has built-in KPIs that help him keep his pulse on the ebb and flow of business. He can notice and face a problem at the first signs.

We will continue to work through Jim's business problems as we progress through the steps: diagnose it, quantify it, treat it, and prevent it.

How would you start to tackle the issues Monroe HVAC is facing?

# Chapter 2

*Running away from a problem*
*only increases the distance from the solution.*
—Anonymous

## DIAGNOSE IT

In the prior chapter, we discussed facing your business problems as the first step in solving and ultimately preventing them. Much of the chapter focused on creating signifiers that will make it possible to quickly identify problems. But once you know something here isn't right (the phone is not ringing with new clients at consistent rates, turnover among certain employees is drastically high), what's the next step? A business owner should then engage in triage. In the medical diagnosis context, triage is the process of determining the priority of patients' treatments by the severity of their condition or likelihood of recovery with or without treatment. In the business setting, it is determining the type of problem, how quickly a problem needs to be handled, and how severe it is. We will take the data gathered from step 1 (Face it), engage in the triage process, and determine what is actually happening and why is it happening. In this stage, we are past just recognizing the problem: "We have high turnover"—that's a symptom. This stage gets us to the root of what is really transpiring.

I can report that I have been to the emergency room four times in my life, three of those times due to the "joys" of entrepreneurship—stress that causes extremely high blood pressure and results in "I think I'm having a stroke. We need to go to the emergency room." When you go to the emergency room, you know the first thing that happens is triage. The level of injury dictates what medical professional you see and how soon you get to see them. Why do medical facilities triage? Because they know they have a lot of people to treat with limited resources, space, and medical professionals to treat them. They also know some individuals come to them that do not need emergency care at all. They also realize that some people come to them having failed to see their primary care doctors in sufficient time. Or they come based on fear that what they are facing is serious, when in fact, time (or a few simple tests) may have revealed to them that it is not. The way that emergency rooms handle the flow of what can be a throng of individuals coming to them is by triage. First, you have to recognize you're injured, and then, based on the information you give at intake, your injury is classified (i.e., triaged). A hospital could maintain no sense of profitability if they brought out their premier board-certified surgeon for every complaint of heart pains. So you triage—a series of questions and exams to get you in the right room and seeing the right people. For your business, triage is asking the right questions to understand what general class of problem you have.

Your business problem-solving process should mirror this. Triage = (1) What type of problem do I have? (2) How quickly does the problem have to be remedied? Every problem is different. Some require all hands on deck, and others may simply require some time to pass. A business operating for six months with one part-time, independent contractor is going to experience different issues than a business operating for twenty years and with 150 employees. Understanding the type of problem you are facing will put you on the road closer to resolution. I have found that there are five major categories of problems a business will face. Of course, this list is not exhaustive, but once you've gathered the information (symptoms from step 1), this list is a good way to start triaging, diagnosing, and categorizing your business problems.

## Types of Problems

1. *Telltale Sign Problems:* This is the most common. This is the problem that is really a symptom of something bigger. It means you're doing something wrong and that if you do not immediately and thoroughly handle it, it will become a bigger issue. Customers routinely returning products or asking for refunds means your policies are not as clear as they should be, and you should spend time revamping the policies as well as how they are communicated to customers. This could also be a sign that your product or service is not as advertised: what your marketing says the product or outcome will be versus what your customer actually experiences or receives doesn't align. You should not take angry customers or clients personally but as an opportunity to improve on what you do. This is where those KPIs we discussed in the last chapter come

into play. Once you have a well-defined system of tracking various performance metrics in your business, these telltale signs will become evident early. Other telltale sign problems include (1) sales routinely down in a certain quarter or month, which could be because your product is seasonal or that in the season or quarter before, you lost steam on marketing efforts, which showed up months later, and (2) employees always call out with unplanned issues and emergencies, which causes issues with workflow. Yes, they could just be horrible employees, but they could also just be burned out, and maybe you need to allow a few more vacation or mental health days for your workforce.

2. ***Pivot Problems***: These are problems that invite you to take a new path in your business. For instance, you have three product lines: Your best seller five years running is starting to take a dive, not significant, but enough to give you pause. The product still gets rave reviews, but why is it selling less? Maybe the market has shifted, or maybe because it sells so well, you've neglected marketing. Maybe it's time to exit selling that product—so this problem could signify a pivot in marketing, market, or what products you sell. I'd submit that every problem is an opportunity to pivot and examine new and better ways to operate. But I would also classify as pivot problems instances where a business needs to make a big leap, such as closing an office, reorganizing staff, or changing product offerings. Here are some examples of pivot problems: (1) option year on a

contract that you were counting on not being exercised or (2) it's clear that your classification of much of your workforce as independent contractors is incorrect given recent court rulings in your state, so now you have to reorganize your workforce and expenses.

3. ***Distraction Problems***: These are annoyances, like a flat tire. Your car works perfectly fine and no one is hurt, but it took time out of your day. Either you had to pull over and take the time to change the tire, or for those who are less inclined in car repair, like myself, you sat, called a tow truck, and they did it. It annoyed you, it cost you some money and time, but you moved on. For a business owner, this is the missed shipment, the payment that's two days late, or the two bad Yelp reviews in a sea of five-star glory—annoying for sure but neither the end of the world or your world and certainly not of your business. Breaches of contract can even be distraction problems if they are small enough. It is horrible to have someone attempt to cheat you out of any amount of money, but you do have to determine if $1,200 is worth fighting over; it may be, but it also may be a distraction from going after more money and bigger clients. Business owners can be prone to spend a lot of time on these distraction problems to the detriment of more pressing issues and opportunities.

4. ***Bet the Company Problems***: These are also problems that started out as telltale problems or even pivot problems, but

you neglected step one (face it) for far too long. Rarely do things spiral out of control in one day or even one month. Bet the company problems—those issues that if not resolved in your favor mean you no longer have a company—include (1) cash flow completely drying up and you will not make payroll this week, (2) your co-founder suing you to strong arm you out of the business, (3) the intellectual property your whole business depends on is smack dab in the middle of litigation and the outcome looks bleak, (4) your whole profit model is based on hiring independent contractors and whether your contractors are more properly classified as employees is before the courts in your state, or (5) you're about to lose that big contract that employs 90% of your workforce (you did not diversity the client base). These are problems that could potentially gut your business or, at best, completely change how you do business.

5. ***You Might Just Need Therapy Problems***: When you— yes, you—are the one and only problem. Now, granted, as a business owner and founder, you permeate the business, and while your identity should not be tied to your business, much of the business's personality will come from your personality, identity, values, and leadership style. You are setting the culture; therefore many parts of your natural disposition may be a part of the company culture and values. If you do not like the current culture or you see it causing myriad issues, be intentional about changing both yourself and

the culture. There are some problems that really are your doing—not the market, not your employees, and not your customers. Only you.

I am not advocating that you dim your personality and do not show up in your business as your authentic self. For many, it was the ability to bring their whole self to their work that drove them to start a business. However, if your natural disposition is to take offense easily and take actions personally, that will be an issue. For instance, any time an employee requests a raise of any amount, you hit the roof. You take it as a slap in the face (How could they not be grateful for their current salary and all I have invested in them?) and contemplate firing the person or, at the least, start micromanaging their every move. Your reaction to their request for a raise, which is quite normal from a business perspective, precipitates more issues. Everything is not a personal affront to your spirit and soul. Also, remember that people's actions very often have little to nothing to do with you personally. You often meet (and perhaps hire) who you are, i.e. what you see in others can often reflect more about you than them, so remember that they are not acting in a certain way because of you but because of them—and you are responding, in whatever way you are responding, because of you, not because of them.

While it is your business—and you get to have your quirks and have things your way—you have to live with the consequences of that. Some business owners like to deal in fear and nasty emails (email thugs is what I call them). This is where self-awareness is key. And if you lack all self-awareness, know enough to surround yourself with advisors and people that will tell you about you.

Many business owners operate in hysterics and assume they're all "Bet the Company Problems." They're not. Most problems are Pivot Problems or Telltale Signs. While Distraction Problems are just that—distractions—you should not ignore them, because they could morph into bigger problems. However, as a business owner, you do have to learn that things will rarely be perfect.

***No Neat Lines:*** Problems will rarely arrange themselves into neat, easy-to-digest categories for your consumption. They will often straddle across one or more categories that need to be tackled in pieces or all at once. They may also operate more like a funnel, with a top-level problem but then narrowing down to other categories of problems that may be less "big" or pressing.

BET THE COMPANY PROBLEMS

PIVOT PROBLEMS

TELLTALE SIGN PROBLEMS

DISTRACTION PROBLEMS

YOU MIGHT JUST NEED THERAPY PROBLEMS

### *Causation:*

So, we've faced the problem, and we've even done some rough categorization into what type of problem it is. But what's the cause? The final step in really diagnosing what the problem is (and key to solving) is determining the cause. Besides facing it, this may very well be the most difficult part for many business owners simply because it's very hard to see yourself sometimes, and the problem may involve some self-introspection. Individuals often spend countless hours in therapy getting to the root of their issues and determining why they act and react in a certain way. Determining the cause of your problem will also involve some level of analysis: self-analysis, purely business, or a mix of both. Much like the types of problems, the cause of the problem could be multiple sources at once.

I alluded to several examples of causes in discussing types of problems. For instance, customers routinely requesting refunds or discounts could be caused by poorly communicated policies or a service or product that has misaligned advertising or delivery. Do your employees always call out with unplanned issues and emergencies, which causes issues with workflow? Perhaps they are bad employees or misaligned with your company. They could also be burned out, and maybe you need to allow a few more vacation or mental health days for your workforce. Or you could allow them time to handle certain personal matters during the workday.

How do we flow from the type of problem to the cause of the problem? Both steps will hinge on much of what we discussed in Chapter 1: systems and processes. Your business will need a method for gathering information and data, which, as we discussed in Chapter 1, can be established by spending time working on the business and developing KPIs. In determining the type of problem, the data will tell you how big of an issue it is for your business. Also, your systems will tell you where things are off and not performing as well, which will lead you to the cause. Business owners, especially seasoned ones, should not discard their instincts at this juncture. Even if the data or people you talk to say one thing, it's okay to rely on your instinct or intuition. For me, as a Christian, this is listening to the Holy Spirit, but generally it's the concept that our decisions may not always make sense or be guided by all of the facts but by a "knowing." In fact, studies have demonstrated that for investors, business owners, managers, and executives, intuition plays an important role in decision making, especially difficult decisions where you cannot see around all of the corners.

In one study of how investors make decisions on where to invest, investors that followed a checklist approach relied on objective business viability data as a point of departure for integrating other data and sought evidence that allowed them to bracket and rationalize downside risk. Alternately, investors that followed a syncopated approach tended toward the perceptions of the entrepreneur to allow them to focus on identifying exceptional investments that could promise to outweigh any risks.

According to the researcher, these findings indicate that investors' "gut feel" is not the impulsive, emotional, and error-prone decision that the dominant judgment and decision-making paradigm sees it as. Instead, it is an elaborate "intuiting process" that uses both emotional and analytical elements without trapping the user in "analysis paralysis" when considering an overwhelming complexity of data.[4]

In another study, the results showed that as the theory predicted, the investors' recommendations prioritized positive assessments of the entrepreneur over weak assessments of the business viability data, indicating that when faced with unknowable risks, formal analytics do not impede experienced investors' intuitive processes.

Overall, the findings showed that the investors used both intuition and formal analysis to develop what they call their "gut feel." Furthermore, the assessments based on their gut feel best predicted their goal of identifying extraordinarily profitable investments and allowed investors to manage situations of unknowable risk.[5]

In this study, the author felt the results showed that intuition was used to some degree by all managers. Moreover, the use of

---

4. Laura Huang, "The Role of Investor Gut Feel in Managing Complexity and Extreme Risk," *Academy of Management Journal*, vol. 61, no. 5 (October 2018): 1821–1847, https://doi.org/10.5465/amj.2016.1009. Using interviews with 110 angel investors, the research found recurring themes that then formed the basis for a model of investors' "gut feel" process.

5. Laura Huang and Jone L. Pearce, "Managing the Unknowable: The Effectiveness of Early-stage Investor Gut Feel in Entrepreneurial Investment Decisions," *Administrative Science Quarterly*, vol. 60, no. 4. (December 2015): 634-670, http://dx.doi.org/10.1177/0001839215597270 Retrieved from https://escholarship.org/uc/item/54j7z903.

intuition increased the higher one was in the company structure, where the problems faced became less predictable.[6]

While completely ignoring data and KPIs is unlikely to be the best approach, as you can see, there is evidence to support an intuitive-based approach to decision making and problem solving.

### *Problems You Can't Diagnose:*

Not being able to diagnose the problem(s) could mean you do not have the right systems in place or have not collected sufficient information. It could mean that you need to go back to the drawing board. It could also indicate that you do not have all of the necessary professionals on board (or the right ones), and that could be the problem in and of itself. Professionals and specialists see trends and facts—patterns that you may not be trained to spot and interpret. A cyber security specialist sees gaps in a company's procedures and technology for securing data. An insurance professional (broker or agent) can tell that you do not have sufficient insurance to cover the universe of losses your particular business may experience. Oftentimes business owners are not aware of the multitude of insurances available to protect their business or the limitations of the insurance they do have. In our cyber security example, the IT specialist can diagnose and mitigate, and the insurance professional can ensure there is insurance for legal costs or business interruption tied to cyber issues. Each of these professionals function together

---

6. Kamila Malewska, "Intuition in Decision Making –Theoretical and Empirical Aspects," *International Journal of Business and Economic Development*, vol. 3 no. 3 (November 2015), https://ijbed.org/cdn/article_file/i-9_c-98.pdf.

to both diagnose and prevent problems. Other professionals that will help you diagnose are CPAs, attorneys, bookkeepers, bankers, human resources professionals, marketing professionals, and public relations professionals. We will expound on the professionals your business may need in the next chapter.

In addition to lacking all of the information or people that could help you diagnose the problem, I again want to point back to our discussion on intuition. This may be an opportunity to stand back and rely on your years of experience to guide you to possible problems when it is not entirely clear what the crux of the issue is.

**Next Steps:** Take one issue you are facing, and categorize it as we have detailed in this chapter. Then start to brainstorm causes using your KPIs.

## "Diagnosing It" in Action

Jim from Monroe HVAC has faced that he has a problem: (1) techs working longer hours than budgeted, (2) not getting enough appointments scheduled each day, and (3) customers starting to complain about wait times. Because Jim spends time working on the business, this piece is fairly straightforward. His KPIs in particular lead him to recognize the issue. His SWOT analysis signals that these are matters to be concerned about. Specifically, Jim knows that one of his possible new competitors, if he expands, has gotten their arrival window down to one hour, and their reviews always point out how timely the tech was and how the customer did not have to waste their whole day waiting on a service professional.

In recognizing that he has a problem, however, he knows it has not morphed into a "bet the company" problem, but it is greater than a distraction. Further, given how widespread it is within each company location and techs, it's not really an interpersonal issue (i.e., his own lack of self-awareness). Jim deduces that this is a telltale sign issue because he knows that the problems speak to greater issues and could impede further growth. As mentioned, Jim has taken several business courses, where he learned the importance of having the right professionals to guide his business—guides who know things the business owner would not have the capacity to. Jim is astute, and early in his business, he assembled a team of professionals to guide him in growing his HVAC empire. Specifically, his accounting department is tracking revenue with respect to wait times and number of appointments; in fact, they are the ones who first flagged the problem. The professionals have told him there is a problem but not what the problem means or why it's happening (i.e., there's another aspect to diagnosing the problem).

How would you categorize Jim's problems, and what are some possible causes?

# Chapter 3

*Whatever you focus your attention on will become*
*important to you even if it's unimportant.*
—Sonya Parker

## QUANTIFY IT

Not everything deserves your attention. Or at least not your full, undivided attention. Even as you organize your day, you have priorities. There are tasks that absolutely have to be done and tasks that are secondary, tasks that you block out two to three hours for and tasks that get a few minutes, if not seconds. Problems are the same way. How much of your time, money, and energy does this problem deserve? Put another way, how many of your resources should you dedicate toward this problem? Quantifying the issue will assist in determining the method needed to solve the problem by posing the following questions: How much and what resources will this problem cost me to solve now? How much if I wait a moderate amount of time, and how much if I wait the longest amount of time possible?

Quantifying and diagnosing are connected steps. Think of diagnosing as Part A and quantifying as Part B. Once both steps are completed, you have a complete diagnosis and likely a prognosis. These steps are separate because you do need some sense of the problem (diagnose) before you can value it (quantify).

For many business owners, quantifying seems counterintuitive because all problems or matters not going as planned seem important and critical. The presence of any areas of deficiency can cause loss of sleep, anxiety, loss of appetite…you know how it goes. If it's a problem that your business is facing, as a business owner, your natural inclination is to desire a path forward and immediate resolution to the exclusion of anything else that may be occurring in your business. So how do you benefit from quantifying? You'd most certainly spend more time, money, and resources fighting a $5 million lawsuit than you would on a small claim for $5,000. While that's an obvious example, quantifying helps you determine how severe the problem is, which will help guide the decision on how much money to spend, what tools to use, and which professionals to engage. When considering the types of professionals their business needs, many businesses owners know they need an accountant and an attorney. They may not know how crucial coaches or insurance brokers are. They know they need a bank but may not realize the importance of a relationship with a banker or several financial institutions.

The question of what professionals to engage is not just a type but also a quality question. You spend more and require greater skill for a higher value problem. It may not be worthwhile to pay a professional $1,000 an hour to solve a problem or consult with you, but if you're facing a $10 million problem and this person has the key, then it does. You get what you pay for is even truer when it comes to the professionals you engage for your business.

Moreover, I often find that business owners do not know specifically what certain professionals do, what problems they solve, or how to use them effectively in their businesses. The following charts break down professionals you will likely need in your business, what function they will serve, how they will function in your business (i.e., what problems the professional will help you solve), and the criteria you should use when selecting.

## ATTORNEY

### FUNCTION

Provide guidance for legal aspects of your business.

### HOW TO WORK WITH

Setting up your business; compliance; drafting and reviewing contracts; advising on employment matters; real estate; leasing; intellectual property; tax issues; disputes; raising capital; acquiring debt.

### SELECTION CRITERIA

Attorneys need to be licensed in the state where they are providing legal guidance; you may also need a specialist specific to your industry, i.e. a health care attorney or governement contracts attorney. These are areas where you should interview multiple candidates for fit and obtain references from successful business owners.

## BOOKKEEPER

### FUNCTION

Record keeping of financial records; records and classifies daily financial transactions of a business.

### HOW TO WORK WITH

Invoicing, accounts receivables, creating basic financial statements such as profit and loss and cash flow.

### SELECTION CRITERIA

They do not require any sort of license: anyone can be a bookkeeper. Find someone experienced in maintaining books for your industry.

## ACCOUNTANT

### FUNCTION

Uses the information generated by the bookkeeper, analyzes information and turns it into various reports to provide guidance to the company.

### HOW TO WORK WITH

Tax planning and advice, creating and implementing financial controls.

### SELECTION CRITERIA

An accountant can provide bookkeeping functions but is typically more costly; they will typically have a degree in accounting or certificate in accounting. You'll want someone knowledgeable who will stay up to date on tax regulations.

## CPA

### FUNCTION

Certified public accountants perform the accounting task described above; if your financial statements need to be audited, a CPA will perform the audit. CPAs also have fiduciary duties to their clients.

### HOW TO WORK WITH

Use as strategic business advisor; tax preparation; financial planning; auditing.

### SELECTION CRITERIA

CPAs are accountants who have passed the CPA exam. You'll want someone knowledgeable who will stay up to date on tax regulations and coursework to maintain the certification.

## BANKER

### FUNCTION

Opening and maintaining accounts, establishing lines of credits; applying for loans.

### HOW TO WORK WITH

They are free strategic advisors that can help with financial planning, taxes, retirement and forecasting. While it won't be as detailed as what an accountant or insurance broker may do, they have a wide range of knowlege that you do not have to pay for.

### SELECTION CRITERIA

Will advocate on your behalf with the bank's underwriters and inform you of banking products that are a good fit for your business.

## FINANCIAL PLANNER

### FUNCTION

Work closely with your accountant and attorney to plan business but also personal finances; this could include insurance, retirement planning, forecasting for future expenditures and hiring.

### HOW TO WORK WITH

They have a bit of a broader view than an acountant or CPA. Utilize your financial planner in strategic planning and forecasting.

### SELECTION CRITERIA

Make sure they do more than just sell insurance; also check their certifications and designations.

## INSURANCE BROKER

### FUNCTION

Insurance brokers represent you and act on your behalf to find the best insurance coverage.

### HOW TO WORK WITH

Brokers will give you deeper advice and they may have greater knowledge across the industry since they work with a lot of insurance carriers.

### SELECTION CRITERIA

Brokers need to be licensed in the state where they are placing coverage; brokerages are not captive, meaning they work across multiple insurance companies. Find out what insurance company they typically place coverage with.

## INSURANCE AGENT

### FUNCTION

Captive insurance agents sell insurance only on behalf of one insurance company; independent agents sell for multiple carriers.

### HOW TO WORK WITH

Advice on what type of insurance you will need and what coverage is typical in your industry.

### SELECTION CRITERIA

Agents need to be licensed in the state where they are placing coverage and and in the specific line: life, auto or general liability.

## EXECUTIVE COACH/BUSINESS COACH

### FUNCTION

This is when you are working on the business and yourself. Setting and achieving goals, keeping you accountable, clearing through mental obstacles to growth, helping you develop strategic business plans (informed by data from the other professionals.)

### HOW TO WORK WITH

Regularly meet and keep him or her appraised on places of improvement, act as a source of objective, and strategic feedback.

### SELECTION CRITERIA

Someone you can relate to with a proven track record of helping similarly situated business owners.

## TRUSTED ADVISORS

### FUNCTION

Act as mentors and advisers.

### HOW TO WORK WITH

Regularly meeting and sharing ideas, resources and business practices; hacking through problems.

### SELECTION CRITERIA

Individuals you trust with proven success in business.

What are some professionals you use, and what was your selection process?

Sometimes the exercise of quantifying is self-explanatory; it would be difficult to justify spending more money to solve a problem than the actual loss to the business. But sometimes it is not that cut and dry. In our lawsuit example, what if the $5,000 lawsuit would result in a judgment against your business that would affect your bonding capacity or losing the lawsuit could mean ten more lawsuits filed on the same basis? You cannot look solely at the value of a problem in a vacuum. You have to quantify with an eye toward what this problem means for your business today but also what it could signal for tomorrow. While money and costs are obvious methods of quantification, another key can be where the problem falls on the scale from simple to chaotic.

In a *Harvard Business Review* article, the authors discuss a framework for categorizing that's illustrative for our purposes of determining how to quantify any problem.[7]

1. ***Simple Problems***: These are problems with clear cause and effect that are pretty clear to anyone. Often the right answer is evident and undisputed. For instance, a simple problem could be that the person in your company that runs payroll is sloppy; the weeks he runs payroll there are always minor errors, with

---

7. David Snowden and Mary Boone, "A Leader's Framework for Decision Making," *Harvard Business Review*, (November 2017), https://hbr.org/2007/11/a-leaders-framework-for-decision-making.

some employees getting paid a few more hours than they actually work. However, the other weeks, when his counterpart runs it, payroll is perfect. The solution is pretty simple: Don't let the sloppy guy run payroll. However, problems can be misclassified as simple because of oversimplification or failure to fully investigate, mainly caused by intellectual laziness. Be certain your simple problem is truly simple. Implement a solution quickly, and if it doesn't work, it could be that your problem was not so simple. But also do your due diligence and evaluate the problem from several angles. In our payroll example, what if payroll is off sometimes because employees are entering their time wrong, they're doing so when they know sloppy guy is running payroll, and it's always the same employees with the extra hours? Well now, that deserves some due diligence and evaluation.

2. *Complicated Problems*: For these problems, while there may be a clear relationship between cause and effect, not everyone can see it. This is where an expert, in consultation with company leaders and the workforce, may be needed to investigate and propose several strategies from not only available options but viable options. Because solving these may involve a team effort involving experts, it may take more time, money, and resources to address these problems. Let's take our payroll example. In the second iteration of the scenario, the same employees are getting paid for hours they did not work when sloppy guy runs payroll. Well, this is complicated. Is there

widespread fraud at the company? Who's involved? Is payroll the only place employees are stealing? There are wage and hour implications in this example. If you start docking pay without proof and they actually worked those hours, then you have stolen from your employees and opened the company up to wage and hour lawsuits, where the penalties are high. You'll need your human resources, accounting, and legal teams to dive into this one. It's certainly complicated.

3.  ***Complex Problems***: Complex problems are the realm of unknown unknowns. Think of it this way: Sports cars are complicated, while the ocean, especially the deep sea, is complex. Often with complex problems, you have to move to one stair for the next stair to illuminate, and you will have to allow solutions to continue to emerge as you move forward, often with uncertainty and perhaps failing as you implement various solutions. In our payroll example, let's make our company a multinational company with employees across the globe. The employment and wage laws vary vastly, so any solution is likely not one size fits all. To make it spicy, let's add in that one of the employees that's being slightly overpaid is in a foreign nation, and his father is a local elected official who's told leaders at your foreign location that if his son were paid a little more each month than he actually worked, he'd be happy to give the company a first look at certain contracts...so now we've stepped into possible violations of the Foreign Corrupt Practices Act in addition to wage and hour violations. Our simple problem is now firmly complex.

4. ***Chaotic Problems***: Chaos is, by definition, unpredictable, unorganized, and utter confusion. Here, just getting things in order, even if the problem isn't solved, may be key. Also key is moving from chaos to at least complex but preferably to complicated. When I think of chaos, what immediately comes to mind is the client juggling multiple complex and complicated problems at once. The mix is chaotic as issues start to overlap, and it is challenging to determine what issues are connected and which are not. You may be tempted to get all hands on deck, but this is where having trusted advisors is instrumental in the success of your business. They will give you objective advice and a starting point from their experience. A clear example of chaos could be our wage and hour issues with the foreign twist, multiple lawsuits, and the departure of high-level management all at one time.

Quantifying helps you assess the impact of the problem or issue on your business. For clarity, each of the types of problems in Chapter 2—telltale signs, pivoting, bet the company, distractions, and therapy needed—can be quantified as listed above. A pivot problem can be simple or part of a chaotic situation, and a telltale problem could be complex or could be simple. In terms of how this helps you quantify, here is one way to assess: A chaotic problem is expensive, not just in the money you may spend to resolve it but also in the effect on every other part of your business, with the money, time, and resources being lost to the chaos. Complex problems are also costly; you have to delve into unknowns given that you may spend significant time or resources to get the business back on an even path. Complicated problems, like complex and chaotic, will generally require a team—so costly in terms of finances. It will consume your time but may not consume you in the same way chaos will.

Quantifying is key to solving because once you have determined the type of problem and the cause of the problem, you have a greater sense of the magnitude and what necessary steps are needed to solve the problem and ultimately prevent future problems.

**Next Steps:**
   (1)   List all of the professionals you currently use.
   (2)   Identify possible gaps in professionals but also their skill sets.

## Quantifying in Action

Remember our friend Jim? Now he has faced that he has a problem: (a) techs working longer hours than budgeted, (2) not getting enough appointments scheduled each day, and (3) customers starting to complain about wait times. In diagnosing, Jim realizes it has not morphed into a "bet the company" problem but rather a "telltale sign" problem. So how does he quantify? We know that he's losing money in the sense that he's not getting the greatest productivity and thereby profitability of his techs. It could be easy to quantify this as "simple," but as we will see, that is certainly an oversimplification and would be the result of a lack of thorough due diligence and evaluation into the problem. It is not a chaotic problem because there are some clear lines to what's happening. Jim is still profitable and has not descended into chaos; business is still steadily moving forward. It is also a stretch to quantify this as complex; while there are unknowns, Jim's systems and processes have already uncovered a lot of data points. But data needs to be analyzed. Given that, I would quantify Jim's problems as "complicated" in that it will take both a team of experts or professionals and his internal team to address. So what does that mean? Jim will have to pay experts, spend time, and expend internal resources to solve the problem. In some respects, since, as we stated, he's still profitable, he could say, "At this moment, perhaps it's not worth tackling this." This approach would not be completely wrong. There are good reasons to procrastinate on solving certain business issues and effective ways to do so. For instance, you may have determined that outdated technology is the source of some of your business problems, but you know it's better financial judgment to wait until a certain quarter to purchase new equipment and know the old equipment will last until then. Jim may want a few more months of data and agrees to check back on the problem in thirty or sixty days. But remember that unresolved complicated issues that linger too long can, with the right trigger, evolve into chaos.

# Chapter 4

*We cannot solve our problems with the same thinking*
*we used when we created them.*
—Albert Einstein

## TREAT IT

So we have arrived at the portion of the book you care most about, probably the reason the title intrigued you and why you picked it up. How do I cure what ails my business? The other steps were vital to get to this point, but it is all for naught if you do not actually resolve the problem. Once you have gone through steps one through three, in many instances, the answer (i.e., what to do) may very well be obvious. While steps one through three are "work," this is the "work" work that may involve some heavy lifting. However, by this point, your anxiety is probably way down. Why? Because not knowing what to do or who to turn to for help is what usually gets your heart racing and causes anxiety, distress, depression, and despair. While doing the work is hard and often outside of your comfort zone, there is peace in knowing what the problem is and just tackling it.

Though not an exact science, your solution will probably lie in the following categories or action items, or multiples thereof:

**Money**

This is fairly intuitive for most business owners. They know the problem will likely require money, a lot or a little, and this knowledge is what forces many to ignore the problem. Really, one should not look at this as spending; it most likely is truly an investment in making your business better. It could mean spending money on new technology, new hires, new marketing campaigns, better insurance policies, or more sophisticated tax planning, which are all investments designed to grow your bottom line by increasing sales or productivity or to secure it by helping you keep more of your profits or lessen the impact of any catastrophe, loss, or lawsuit—provision and protection.

A financial planner that specializes in working with small businesses informed me that the biggest mistake he sees business owners make is not paying themselves and not insuring themselves and their business. This spend is key—protection and provision. You have to keep yourself adequately incentivized as a business owner, and you want to protect the asset. The business is the asset, but so are you. Also, if you're an employee of your S Corp business, you are required to pay yourself an adequate salary to remain compliant and avoid an audit.

Quite frankly, I cannot think of any problem that will not involve spending money or cutting spending to some extent. You have to appreciate that any time you spend away from doing the thing your business does to make money means you are spending your precious time (the equivalent of money) on the problem. There is always a time–money element to consider.

The solution may not just be purely spending money. It could be that you need to keep expenses in check by downsizing staff or reducing expenses. As you begin to grow, naturally your expenses will increase as well. (Spending money makes you money. That may sound counterintuitive, but you know it's true.) Keeping an eye on expenses is not simply tracking how much the business is spending on payroll; it means that you are monitoring proper staffing and how profitable each employee is. If you're monitoring, you'll be more likely to move faster on moving unproductive staff members to other positions or terminating them. In addition to "right sizing" staff, this will increase your profit margin and cash flow, which invariably could solve several problems at once. It could also be that you need to borrow money or obtain a line of credit in order to increase your cash flow. Many bankers and financial planners will tell you that cash is king. For many businesses, it's the flow of the cash that causes the issues and the ultimate consequences of those issues, such as not being able to pay employees (stiff fines and penalties from government), not being able to pay vendors or contractors (legal action, they stop working or supplying), and unable to adequately forecast and spend on marketing (decreased sales), hampering the growth you need to—you guessed it—increase cash flow.

## People

Many business owners say that having to wear all the hats in the business is one of the most challenging aspects. You are the chief strategy officer, marketer, human resources director, administrator, bookkeeper, and lead salesperson. If you have gone it completely alone, this could be part of the problem. When I first started my law firm as a solo practitioner, a federal judge, who had previously had his own firm prior to being appointed to the bench, said, "While you may be solo, you are not alone." Even if you run a micro operation, the solution could be to outsource certain aspects of your business. Your cash flow could be causing a domino effect of issues, but the problem is you are responsible for doing the work, sending the invoice, and following up on the invoice. Those last parts may take a back seat to doing the work. You may need to either outsource or build your internal team. I once heard a popular celebrity hairstylist say, "If you can carry the money bag by yourself, it's not big enough." Problems that require hiring could be backlogs in work, which, in turn, mean lags and backlogs in collecting payments and certain things just not getting done in the business, such as compliance and tax matters.

Or perhaps you have people, even good people, just not the right people. Sometimes you do have to move the good people to get to the right people. In the first few years in business, you may be tempted just to put bodies in seats and not hire for fit, culture, and values. You need a strong sense of your culture and values before you can begin hiring employees that have the skills but also fit within your company ethos.

Sometimes it is obvious when to let go of a person on your team: They have stopped performing, they do not show up on time or at all, and the thing you hired them to do is not getting done. Other times it is not as obvious when to let an employee go. They may be likeable and have a great attitude, but perhaps the employee or contractor lacks the skill set necessary, or your business is evolving and they do not have the capacity to go to the next level with you. If you still feel like you have to do everything (sucking away time from you being CEO, truly managing, and spending time working on the business), you may not have the right individuals. Letting go of employees in the first few years in business is always hard. I notice the first termination is specifically hard for some business owners. If you have a small team, this person has likely become your friend, and you know lots of details about each other's lives. It is difficult to terminate people you've developed a connection with.

Collaborations or joint ventures may also lead to the skill sets, people, or capacity you need in your business. This entails two or more entities coming together for a common goal. The joint venture could be for a short period of time, a specific project, or longer in duration and cover particular types of opportunities. The businesses could decide to enter into a contract that describes the scope of the arrangement, or the joint venture could create a new entity altogether for a specific project or new business certifications. Many business owners have informed me that collaborations and partnerships were key to their success and one of the best parts of being in business. Your issue could be consistently missing big opportunities that could catapult your business (and increase cash flow! Pattern anyone?). A joint venture could bring that added skill set or even perspective that your proposals are missing.

## Process and Systems (Improving or Creating)

We have talked about this throughout the duration of the book. If you take anything away from this book, it should be this! You need systems and processes. You need to monitor them, and you have to refine and improve them over time. Every problem in your business is very likely the result of a breakdown in a process or a lack of one: (1) consistently unpaid invoices, (2) employees violating the same policies, or (3) missed service or product delivery deadlines. These all involve policy, procedure, and process.

## Business Model & Profit Model

In many ways, these go hand in hand and, in simple terms, refer to a company's plan for making a profit. You may not have a strong sense of the company's real value proposition. Also knowing what's profitable in your business is crucial data. Your team may be spending time, money, and resources on items that are not profitable, or the effort is not aligned with the level of profit. This is where you have to spend time in the business evaluating the bottom line. Problems that require changes to business or profit model include service or product lines that are not profitable (tracking this requires—you guessed it—financial controls to measure profitability) and spending a lot of time or money correcting orders or responding to customer complaints about service or product quality.

## Branding & Marketing

Branding and marketing are often used interchangeably, and if you are using them to mean the same thing, that may be the problem your business is facing. Think of branding as your business identity and marketing as the methods that you use to communicate that business identity to your customers and competitors. Branding is who your customers say you are, and marketing is how they find you.

It could be that what you say you do and what the market thinks you do are two different things.

One of my clients has consistently great reviews across multiple platforms; her customers are saying exactly what she wants them to say about the business (i.e., her brand terms show up in the reviews). For instance, they want to be seen as knowledgeable, and the review says, "They seemed to have in-depth knowledge on…." This is not a coincidence. She was intentional about her brand and how she wanted customers to describe the business. She formed focus groups to inquire about needs and what people wanted out of this particular type of business; she took their exact words and used them in her marketing and other aspects of her company and created a culture that embodied what her customers were seeking.

With respect to marketing, you may not be showing up in the right "channels" with consistency. Marketing is not a one-time event; it requires you to have your message on repeat. Think of how frequently some TV and radio ads play. Moreover, there are so many types of marketing—social media, print, TV, radio—but do not forget relationship marketing. Your best customers are always the customers you already have. And those current customers are the best sources of referrals for new customers. Problems that change marketing and branding efforts include consistently being asked to perform services that you believe you have not advertised and your business is always "under capacity." For a product-based business, this could be having surplus inventory; for a service-based business, it is not being able to keep you or your staff on money-generating activities.

## Put It in Writing

Business can happen at a fast pace. You have an idea, and the next thing you know, you have several customers and are building the plane as you are flying it. Business owners can operate for years without the proper agreements between founders and a customer agreement they got from Google or a friend with a completely different type of business. You will not know these things are a problem or the documents are defective until there is a problem and you have to rely on the written agreement to guide the dispute. You will not realize your own agreement bound you to arbitration in Nevada even though you and most of your customers are in Florida. Getting a solid set of documents that you understand will solve (and prevent) a plethora of issues. Problems that may stem from lack of proper agreements include you and your business partner having disputes around decision making in certain key areas or several employees leaving and trying to take your clients, documents, or proprietary information with them. Another common problem is signing something that's pretty explicit, but because of what the other party said, you operate as if the very clear terms do not really mean anything. The other party to the contract may be benevolent, but when the rubber hits the road, they will rely on a strict interpretation of the contract. Further, most agreements have terms that essentially say, "Anything we said prior to this doesn't count and isn't binding unless it's in this document, and if we were to change anything, it would be in writing and not orally."

For some, going through this list may make them retreat and not do anything. Often we know what to do; we just don't do it. So we are again at Step 1: Facing It. Going through the analysis may make some feel "failure" (i.e., how could I miss that or how could I let it get that bad)?. But think of it all as practice, which is really just controlled failure. You will make mistakes, so let them make you into a better business owner.

As we discussed in Chapter 2, the diagnosis will rarely occupy clean lines and one category. In law school, they teach "issue spotting" of certain facts you know will give rise to certain legal issues. And you compare and contrast the present circumstance with a prior circumstance as a guide for the outcome. It's the same for doctors; certain illnesses present themselves in a certain manner, which helps physicians diagnose and then offer the best course of treatment.

**Next Steps:**
Think about current issues and possible categories for solutions.

## Treating It in Action

Using the KPIs he implemented, Jim has faced that he has the following problems: (1) techs working longer hours than budgeted, (2) not getting enough appointments scheduled each day, and (3) customers starting to complain about wait times. This is a telltale problem that we have quantified as more than likely to be complicated in that it will take both a team of experts or professionals as well as his internal team to address and solve. Let's go through the categories of solutions we discuss in this chapter to see what may work best for Jim:

1. *People Problems*: Problems 1 and 2 (which are leading to problem #3) could be a function of who he's hiring. While the first instinct could be that we just have bad employees, that may not be the whole truth. This is especially true since it's an issue across the company at several Monroe HVAC locations and not just a few bad apples. Between Jim's team of experts and his internal team, they begin to brainstorm the topic. (Getting everyone in the room to discuss the issue really is crucial. There's no shortage of good ideas that come from a well-put-together team. If you've gleaned anything in these pages, I hope it's that you cannot go on this journey alone and get very far.) One of Jim's trusted advisors is Rochelle; she owns a cleaning franchise with three locations. He met her in one of his CEO groups, and she's been in business about three years longer than Jim. While cleaning and HVAC are very different, appointment win-

dows and staffing are quite similar. Rochelle asks about Jim's hiring process, onboarding, written expectations for techs, and whether newly hired techs shadow more senior employees—essentially, how do his hires know how to do things "the Monroe HVAC way"? Jim knows that the occasionally outsourced appointments are certainly not done in the Monroe way. Jim further knows it would be difficult to get a third party to agree to train his team a certain way for so few appointments. Internally, Jim has always been so concerned with the techs' skill set and proper certifications—making certain his techs conduct themselves in accordance with certain standards or a company ethos has been something he's thought of and talked about with staff—but he has never really built any systems and processes, which takes us to the next category.

2. *Process and Systems*: Many business owners are so concerned with finding the right talent and putting them to work to generate revenue that they step over the whole onboarding process. I'm not talking about filling out forms and selecting insurance but rather integrating them into the organization. This is especially key as it relates to Jim's techs as they don't work in an office setting, so it's easy for them to really act like lone wolves on the job. Onboarding is not a one-day conversation but really a process that can take several months of an employee's tenure and is an ongoing process. Studies have shown a positive correlation between

profitability and customer ratings (all issues Jim is concerned with) and employee engagement.[8]

So we know Jim is an astute businessman, but he's not an HR professional—this is where you tap into the team. Jim takes advice from Rochelle to meet with his HR director and Chief Operations Officer (who is actually Jim's wife), and because a plethora of employee laws are implicated, Jim brings in his employment attorney. In brainstorming ideas, the team Jim assembles realizes there's a missing component and a skill set they all have but really need outside guidance on: developing his company mission, vision, and beliefs. While he knows what they are internally, Jim does not have an effective way of conveying that outside of his own brain. While the team could draft this on their own, a strategic planner or even an executive coach could help them finetune this. Onboarding employees into these foundational beliefs is key as you create an invested workforce that understands the implications of not getting enough appointments finished in a day and working longer hours than the company has budgeted for.

So we see that for Jim, "People" includes better training of his current staff and bringing in a strategic planner to help solidify the company's mission, vision, and values (MVV). The MVV would be conveyed to his corporate team and incorporated into how Monroe HVAC does business. Think Chick-fil-A and how their company values are really baked into every step of their customer process.

---

8. Understanding Employee Onboarding, Society for Human Resource Management, assessed May 13, 2023, https://www.shrm.org/resourcesandtools/tools-and-samples/toolkits/pages/understanding-employee-onboarding.aspx.

1. ***Business Model***: There could be services offered that are both unprofitable and time consuming. Eliminating these could make an immediate impact on scheduling and how many hours his techs work. Focusing on the business model may be a quicker solution than revamping the onboarding process. If I were advising Jim, I'd say it's not a zero sum game; you can simultaneously implement solutions. This could be a quick fix, while the focus on integrating his employees is part of the long-term strategic plan.

2. ***Branding & Marketing***: Jim's problem appears to be internal and spilling into the external, so the solution may not be here. However, any good branding expert will tell you how crucial your mission, vision, and values are to your brand. Your MVV is what you communicate to clients. It's both internal (employee buy-in to the MVV and resulting processes) and

external (communicated to customers). As such, the natural iteration would be to find ways to ensure once he's revamped his mission, vision, and values, that's communicated to customers through marketing.

3. ***Put It in Writing***: Once the new onboarding policies are inked, getting his employees to sign an acknowledgment of having gone through various components during the process is important. One other wrinkle could be terminating the contract with the third-party company Jim occasionally uses for overflow work. The contract is pretty loose, and the two owners drafted it themselves without attorney review or oversight. There are contract nuances that can often be overlooked when not properly vetted (i.e., notice prior to termination, does termination have to be for cause, is there a termination fee, can the third-party solicit Jim's customers, can Jim hire the other company's employees).

4. ***Money***: None of this is free. Jim has to pay his attorney and the strategic planner. And his staff now have to focus on this new initiative, which has a cost element in that his employees' time is not on whatever else used to fill their day; he may have to pay overtime or even incentivize the planning staff with a bonus.

By implementing each of these steps, Jim will start achieving greater efficiency, all for the end game of not only making more money but having more engaged staff and thus less employee turnover, which, in turn, results in better revenue over time. Jim probably will feel empowered to think expansion and franchising as we have developed a method that can then be duplicated many times over without diluting his hard-earned reputation in the business.

# Chapter 5

*A prudent person with insight foresees danger coming and
prepares himself for it but the senseless
rush blindly forward and suffer the consequences.*
—Proverbs 22:3 (TPT)

## PREVENT IT

Prevent probably is not the ideal word. You can get a flu shot, eat
healthy, religiously wash your hands, and still get the flu. One can
never fully prevent problems; a flu shot is crisis anticipation (flu
season is upon you and can suck days, if not weeks, from an otherwise productive, healthy life) and risk management (a flu shot,
and other acts can lessen the chance you get the flu). Clients often
lament that they want a bullet-proof contract so that suppliers or
customers cannot sue them, or they want an ironclad operating
agreement to control any rogue partners or even an employee
handbook that will keep employees in line and fully eliminate any
personnel issues. While these mechanisms go a long way toward
giving you peace of mind, regulating and dictating behavior, and
providing a framework if there is a problem, they simply cannot
prevent them. Why? Because people…well, they're people! We
can be irrational creatures, and you simply cannot stop that. If you
have lived even a bit of life, you have been utterly surprised by the

actions of what otherwise appear on the surface to be lovely and sane individuals.

While there are rules to punish folks if they file a frivolous lawsuit, that does not mean they will not do it. While you and your partner agreed to manage the business a certain way, it does not mean life circumstances cannot make them flip the script. You may consistently train your employees to not harass each other (which seems simple and intuitive) but still get complaints of various forms of harassment between employees or between employees and customers. To some extent, this is not something you can prevent; being in business means you will encounter problems, even without your doing and even if you do every single thing right or as close to right as possible. For instance, even a change in legislation can wreak havoc. And hackers are always searching for their next victim.

So while this chapter is entitled "Prevent It," it is probably best conceptualized as "crisis anticipation" and "risk management." We cannot eliminate all trace of problems in your business (or even your life), but we can anticipate, manage, and build organizational resilience to handle what may come your way.

## Crisis Anticipation

One of Merriam-Webster Dictionary's definitions of crisis is "an unstable or crucial time or state of affairs in which a decisive change is impending." Anticipation is defined as "the act of looking forward." If we dig a lot deeper into the biblical (Greek) definition of crisis, or krisis in Greek, it is related to the word "judgment," or a divine sentence or decision. The biblical (Greek) definition of anticipation, *phtanō*, refers to prevention or doing beforehand. Taking the sum of both definitions, crisis anticipation refers to being prepared beforehand for a time that will require decisions and changes.

Crisis anticipation makes me think of a guard standing watch over a castle. It could be a quiet day, or it could be one filled with turmoil. Either way, the guard, though perhaps seeming unassuming and unengaged, is actively on the lookout for signs of discord or danger and lives in a state of anticipation. You should be that way in your business. I'm not saying expect bad things to happen, but I am expressing that you should put systems and processes in place so you can easily see danger on the horizon: (1) create systems, (2) spend time working on the business, (3) establish key indicators, (4) listen to your customers, (5) embrace difficult conversations, and (6) create an emotional support system (i.e., create a watchman). Thinking about it in terms of crisis anticipation is the natural progression of the watchman you've developed.

The time you spend assessing strengths and weaknesses will illuminate potential pitfalls and, more importantly, increase your self-awareness.

### Assemble Your Crisis Anticipation Team

Assemble your crisis anticipation team regularly. This is every professional we listed in the chart in Chapter 2. Regularly talking to this team, and having them talk to each other, is the first step in anticipating. Experts have to know what you're doing to advise you. While many business owners do engage in somewhat regular conversations with certain professionals, getting them all together to brainstorm all things related to your business may be less intuitive. Each of the professionals listed will function in the present or even in the past (i.e., giving you advice on a problem that is currently happening). The key is to find professionals with the skill set and experience that will help you look into the future.

## Auditing

While a tax or financial audit instinctively makes sense to many business owners, the audit process can be applied to every function in your business. In my law firm, I refer to them as "legal checkups," where I take a deep dive into the client's legal documents and every legal aspect of their business: think hiring materials, employee handbooks, privacy policies, customer contracts, billing policies—anyplace where there may be legal exposure. I assess my client's risks and develop a plan for what needs to get done and how urgently. You can apply this to multiple functions in your business with applicable trusted professionals: tax payments, human resources, marketing, banking, operations, and technology. A marketing audit may entail taking a deep dive into all of your assets—website, ads, newsletter—looking at calls and conversion rates, and reviewing marketing regulations that may be pertinent to your industry marketing spend.

There are at least two immediate benefits to both auditing and assembling the team: You may realize that some of the situations are preventable by simply modifying existing methods of operation. You can also begin to think about possible responses and about best-case/worst-case scenarios, etc. Better now than when under the pressure of an actual crisis. In some cases, of course, you know a crisis will occur because you're planning to create it (i.e., laying off employees or making a major acquisition).

## Risk Management

Risk management is the active implementation of the data you learned from your crisis management team and audit process and putting it into an active plan for your company. You have discovered the risk, so now what? In my legal checkup example, risk management is the second part of the checkup: creating a plan to implement from the data collected. Most Fortune 500 companies have large risk management departments, or they hire the top consulting firms for particularly thorny risk management issues; think KPMG or Deloitte. Yes, you are a small business, but yes, you, too, should have a risk management department, even if it's a department of one (you) and your outside professionals. Typically, the focus of corporate risk management departments is to prevent financial losses across all segments of business. Because reputational harm often leads to financial losses, the risk management department must be multi-disciplinary and understand all the business systems and processes.

For your business, risk management should include the following areas:

### 1. *Insurance*

Insurance in general is a contract, a promise by the insurance company to cover a loss. For business, the most common type of insurance that will cover the majority of your losses is commercial general liability insurance, or CGL, sometimes referred to as a business owner's policy. The main insuring clause of a CGL policy typically states the following:

> We will pay those sums that the insured becomes legally obligated to pay as damages because of "bodily injury," "property damage," or "personal and advertising injury" to which this insurance applies. We will have the right and duty to defend the insured against any "suit" seeking those damages. However, we will have no duty to defend the insured against any "suit" seeking damages for "bodily injury," "property damage" or "personal and advertising injury" to which this insurance does not apply. (Hartford Policy)

There's a lot that is said in the insuring clause and a lot that it does not say. It does provide that if you have damage to your building or products you sell; someone in your business is hurt; customers are injured; or something you say in advertising your business means you get a demand letter, investigated, or sued, the insurance company will cover the loss and also pay attorney fees. However, the key to the insurance policy is not what it covers but what it explicitly excludes. You want to make sure you understand what it covers but also what it doesn't so you have a plan for that particular loss, if that is a risk for your business. For instance, most policies will exclude any intentional act. The policy I just quoted from excludes wage and hour claims (claims that you have misclassified employees or not properly paid them). This is not an uncommon claim or loss for many businesses, especially small ones that overly rely on independent contractors. As such, as a business owner, you have to find another way to manage this risk, which we will discuss when we talk about compliance. This policy also excludes nuclear energy liability, a loss many small businesses are unlikely to incur.

It's important to take your crisis anticipation data (team + audit) and use it to assess risks, whether those risks are insurable, and, if they are, whether you want to insure them. While you may choose not to insure, this brings certain risk. However, even if you do not have certain insurance, in reality you do—you've chosen (consciously or not) to self-insure. Some companies are purposely self-insured for a variety of reasons, mainly stemming from the cost of the insurance versus the likelihood of the loss or that they can't get insured for a particular loss. For instance, British Petroleum (remember the Gulf of Mexico oil spill?) is mostly self-insured because the premiums for an oil company, where losses for oil spills are often in the billions, do not make economic sense for the company to pay and, quite frankly, may not even be available.

For your business, this is where your insurance broker/professional becomes critical in assessing risk, understanding available insurance coverage, and performing a cost benefit analysis for the insurance. Types of insurance to consider for your business include (1) life, (2) disability, (3) health, (4) professional liability, (5) commercial general liability, (6) employment practices, (7) cyber, (8) auto, (9) errors and omissions, (10) directors and officers, (11) workers' compensation, (12) property, and (13) key employee insurance (aka key man insurance).

## 1.  *Contracts and Contract Management*

We've discussed this throughout the book. Contracts are key for your business and definitely crucial to managing risk. Contracts are preventative medicine. Businesses get in trouble by not having them and, more importantly, by not understanding what they have signed or what they are requiring others to sign. Contracts mitigate risk in a myriad of ways but some key ways to consider are 1) prescribing what to do if there is a dispute (good faith, negotiation, mediation, arbitration, or which court to go to) and 2) shifting certain risk between parties with indemnity clauses. Indemnity is essentially when one party agrees to pay for potential losses or damages caused by another party. One way to think of this is one party is in a superior position to control the risk, so then they should cover or insure it. Here's a typical indemnity clause in a subcontracting agreement:

> Subcontractor, at its own expense, agrees to indemnify, defend, and hold Company and its officers, directors, employees, and agents free and harmless from all claims, demands, losses, costs, expenses, obligations, liabilities, damages, recoveries, and deficiencies, including interest, penalties,

attorneys' fees, and costs that Company may incur as a result of a breach by Subcontractor of any representation or agreement contained in this agreement or in connection with any act or omission of Subcontractor in connection with the provisions of the services hereunder.

It's easy to find sample contracts and contract terms online. You'll be tempted to copy them verbatim, but don't. There are so many ways to draft contracts and contract terms, so you have to be certain your sample even applies to your situation. Do not assume that it does just because it contains a few of your key terms.

### 2.  *Compliance*

Business compliance really just means, are you following all laws and regulations relevant to your business? Not doing so can mean legal exposure and also investigation from government agencies with the power to implement hefty fines. There are many areas of compliance to consider and probably more than you could imagine, so building a strong system to ensure you are compliant is important. Part of this is definitely relying on the teams and professionals we have discussed and empowering them in their zones of genius. Building the teams to handle crises, auditing, risk management, and contract compliance are all steps that get you to what will ultimately be your business compliance plan. There are internal compliance matters to consider—matters related to your own record keeping, such as documenting major corporate decisions with resolutions—and external matters, such as ensuring business certifications are maintained or that annual or biennial reports have been filed in states where you have organized the business or registered as a foreign entity. These are simple ways business owners get tripped up. You go to execute bank documents, and you do not have the proper resolutions/consents or your entity is not in good standing because you failed to file the proper reports. Simple reports and documents left unfiled and attended to can cause major delays, problems, and fees.

Consider the following items to add to your compliance check-list. This list is by no means exhaustive, and it has to be specific to your business—for instance, if you have temporary or seasonal employees or if you have operations in multiple states, your list will be different—and account for the various jurisdictions where you operate.

☑ Employees (Hiring, Pay and Leave)
- ☑ Employees paid on time
- ☑ Time and leave recordation
- ☑ Employees given the proper number of breaks and leave
- ☑ Pay rate compliant with applicable laws

☑ Employee (Benefits & Record Keeping)
- ☑ Workers Compensation
- ☑ Health Insurance
- ☑ Cobra
- ☑ From 1-9

☑ Reporting (State and Regulatory)
- ☑ Franchise Tax
- ☑ Annual or Biennial Report
- ☑ Industry Specific (for instance if you run a nursing home or day care, you may have obligations to report suspected abuse or neglect)

☑ Licensing
- ☑ Business license to operate in your state or county
- ☑ Industry specific (beauty and grooming; day care; health care etc.)

☑ Corporations
- ☑ Meeting minutes
- ☑ Resolutions
- ☑ Officers and board members elected

☑ LLC, Partnerships
- ☑ Resolutions

The key thing to remember is this is not "I've done it, so it's done." Most of the areas listed (which is not an exhaustive compliance checklist) have to be renewed or reviewed yearly or when there is a change in regulation.

### 3. *Business Continuity Planning*

There are some things your business simply cannot anticipate—COVID, anyone?—but beyond pandemics, there are natural weather disasters, terror events, government shutdowns, data breaches, and power outages. These are problems you certainly are not equipped to control and will hardly receive advance warning for...but you can plan for. A business continuity plan outlines how a business will continue operating during an unplanned disruption in service. Business continuity means you can get back to your business operations soon after an unplanned event. Part of the plan will include disaster recovery (i.e., backup and retrieval of your data, servers, software, mobile devices, and documents).

The other part of the plan is creating a system for continuous operations, which could include ensuring all employees are equipped to work from home, phones can easily be diverted, you have access to a backup space to work, key documents are backed up and easily accessible, and you have a proven method to quickly communicate with both your teams and your customers. The most important part of the plan is likely going to be the individuals you've tapped to be the leads for certain parts of the plan and to implement certain parts of it. Finally, you'll want to test your plan, like a fire drill. If you remember these from your school days, the fire drill tested the actual alarm, provided a run-through of everyone leaving the building and getting to the planned location, and ensured that the leaders had everything running smoothly. The same is true for your continuity plan: stress testing your networks, document storage, and the technology that enables your staff to work from home and ensuring your leaders are equipped to activate the plan when needed.

### 4. Succession Planning

If you think of your business as an entity that can and will live on without you, it will help frame the discussion for succession planning. While that may not be what you want—you may want it to die when you die—you still have to plan for that. Succession planning is essentially creating an exit strategy for your business, either because of death, retirement, disability, or simply a desire to move on or business partners desiring to move on from each other. If building something that lasts is your desire, you most certainly will need a plan. Studies show that 70% of businesses fail as they move from the first to the second generation of owners. Only about 15% are successfully transferred to a third generation of family members.

Succession planning matters because these are areas that cause massive, expensive problems for businesses. Partnership disputes, or disputes between heirs of a business owner, often result in complete collapse of the business. Once these issues end up in court, they are expensive, drawn out, and time consuming. If you are spending a significant amount of time on a problem, you lose time toward actually running the business and generating money.

One of my friends is a litigator who handles quite a bit of what's referred to as partner divorces (which is exactly how it sounds: two partners separating and finding ways to divide assets or buy out a partner). I asked her what business owners could have in their foundational documents (shareholder agreements, buy-sell agreements, partnership agreements, etc.) that could help with these disputes. Her answer shocked me: "Well, if they had agreements at all, they'd be in infinitely better positions..." I cannot stress enough how priceless planning in this area is, not only for problems but the good stuff that happens: loans, investments from third parties, or acquiring real estate from your business. You may think splitting from your business partner, who is your bestie, cousin, significant other, or husband, is far-fetched. You love this person, and you get along so well. All of that is probably true...today, but motivations change. I have seen with my own eyes people resent and hate loved ones they went into business with. You do not have to assume the worst, but assume that people grow over time, and you and your business partner may just want different things in the future.

A good succession plan is complicated and outside the scope of this book; it involves shareholder agreements, partnership agreements, and buy-sell agreements but also wills, trusts, life insurance, valuations, human resources, and tax questions. This is where that team we've discussed comes in; this is part of their job as well. A succession plan will be specific to each business, type of business, and, more crucially, business owner.

## Building Organizational Resilience

Much like individual resilience, organizational resilience asks the question, do you have the ability to recover from or adjust to change and/or unfortunate circumstances? When COVID first hit, this became super evident—who's household was ready with supplies (toilet paper), savings, and really the mental fortitude to move through the rapid changes that were happening in our collective world. For your organization, this is almost every concept we have discussed in this chapter but also this book—having systems and processes in place to prevent or easily detect problems and having a strong organizational culture. What do we believe, why do we do what we do, and what's our unique way of doing it? Also, implementing standard rules you can apply when situations are not predictable—we only take on these types of projects, we work with these agencies, we invest in these types of projects only—means your business has a strong sense of identity and can realign quickly when things feel chaotic.

In addition to organizational resilience, build your resilience as the owner. When we talked about facing your problems in Chapter 1, developing an emotional support system was one key. Simultaneously owning and running a business, ensuring profits are met, managing employees and customer expectations, and forecasting and planning for the future is hard. What you do is hard. You need to have resilience. Tap into your faith and spiritual practices, maintain a balanced diet, move your body, engage with friends and family in meaningful ways, lean on mentors, and see your therapist regularly. All of these things build resilience.

How? Because you're the person your organization can lean on for these things in times of chaos. You have created routines, habits, and mindsets that can be steady when you don't have a single clue what's around the corner.

**Next Steps:**
    (1)   Develop an audit checklist process.
    (2)   Brainstorm ways to create personal and organizational resilience.

## Preventing It in Action

As we have discussed, for Jim, this is a bit of a misnomer. One can never really prevent problems in life or in business. If you own a business, you will experience problems. Jim has a really good foundation however. The first step was developing metrics that he keeps his finger on. This allows him to prevent the problem from becoming exasperated. While Jim should be certain to implement all of the elements from our discussion on preventing it, Monroe HVAC will benefit greatly from auditing to prevent future problems, especially problems similar to the ones we've discussed.

For Monroe HVAC, auditing will entail gathering his team of professionals and having them perform audits on various aspects of the business. His HR team can develop methods to audit how effectively they are onboarding hires into the "Monroe HVAC Way." This will likely include obtaining customer feedback as well. The audit process should be developed for each area of the business: sales, marketing, contract management, and operations. These areas will, in some respects, overlap with each other, with one area undoubtedly informing another (for instance, a marketing audit will reveal great insight for the sales team). Auditing does not have to be done all the time; even yearly mini audits will go a long way toward prevention of problems. In Jim's scenario, an audit of his marketing or even operations may have revealed he was missing a robust MVV, which is key in solving Monroe HVAC's initial problems.

# Conclusion

Effective problem solving is a skill you can learn. Over time you can work to develop tools and methods that work not only for your business but for your personality and work style—tools that will help you work through the challenges your business will undoubtedly face. And when things happen, rely on those. As you know, it's very hard to build a foundation or house in a storm—not impossible, just hard.

While this book is clear that I am a proponent of effective problem solving, I am not telling you to worry about what's to come. Worry puts you in a future that has not happened. There's a pretty big black line between planning and stewarding what you have versus simply worrying about the future. Do not let the news, other people, or anything else drive you to fear as it relates to your business. The news will never be all good. It's not their job to tell you all good news; they wouldn't make money that way. It is your job to seek out solid information as it relates to your business and industry, to plan, to organize, to hire the right professionals, to seek good counsel, and to do what you can to shore up the ship for storms.

(1) Face It
(2) Diagnose It
(3) Quantify It
(4) Treat It
(5) Prevent It

# References

Cardon, Melissa S. and Pankaj C. Patel. "Is Stress Worth it? Stress-related Health and Wealth Trade-offs for Entrepreneurs." *Applied Psychology*, (2013): 64.

Freeman, Michael A. M.D., Sheri L. Johnson, Ph.D., Paige J. Staudenmaier, and Mackenzie R. Zisser. "Are Entrepreneurs "Touched with Fire"? *(pre-publication manuscript)*, https://michaelafreemanmd.com/, (2015).

Huang, Laura. "The Role of Investor Gut Feel in Managing Complexity and Extreme Risk." *Academy of Management Journal*, vol. 61, no. 5 (October 2018): 1821–1847, https://doi.org/10.5465/amj.2016.1009.

Huang, Laura and Jone L. Pearce. "Managing the Unknowable: The Effectiveness of Early-stage Investor Gut Feel in Entrepreneurial Investment Decisions." *Administrative Science Quarterly*, vol. 60, no. 4 (December 2015): 634-670, http://dx.doi.org/10.1177/0001839215597270 Retrieved from https://escholarship.org/uc/item/54j7z903.

Malewska, Kamila. "Intuition in Decision Making–Theoretical and Empirical Aspects." *International Journal of Business and Economic Development*, vol. 3 no. 3 (November 2015): https://ijbed.org/cdn/article_file/i-9_c-98.pdf.

Snowden, David and Mary Boone. "A Leader's Framework for Decision Making." *Harvard Business Review*, (November 2017: https://hbr.org/2007/11/a-leaders-framework-for-decision-making.

Witters, Dan, Sangeeta Agrawal, and Alyssa Davis. "Entrepreneurship Comes With Stress, But Also Optimism." *Gallup*, last modified December 7, 2012. https://news.gallup.com/poll/159131/entrepreneurship-comes-stress-optimism.aspx.

"Understanding Employee Onboarding." Society for Human Resource Management, assessed May 13, 2023. https://www.shrm.org/resourcesandtools/tools-and-samples/toolkits/pages/understanding-employee-onboarding.aspx.

# About the Author

S havon J. Smith is the founding partner of The SJS Law Firm, serving as fractional general counsel to businesses in Washington D.C. and Maryland. As an attorney and advisor for nearly two decades—both at a large corporate firm and in her own practice—Shavon understands her job is part-*corpus juris* and part-psychological. Clients often come to her when their problems are already out of hand.

Whether caused by denial, overwhelm, or total system breakdown, runaway problems can be disastrous to a small business. Shavon is committed to helping entrepreneurs create the organizational infrastructure to face, solve, and prevent problems, which will ultimately lead to stronger businesses and more resilient communities.

In her free time, she teaches entrepreneurship at Prince George's County Community College, sits on the nonprofit board of Wheeler Creek Community Development Corporation, and serves on the Pro Bono Committee for the D.C. Bar. She regularly lectures at the American Bar Association, various Chambers of Commerce, Prince George's County Economic Development Corporation, National Society of Black Engineers, and District of Columbia Women's Bar Association, among others.

Shavon holds a J.D. from Howard University School of Law, and previously clerked for Judge Anna Blackburne-Rigsby on the District of Columbia Court of Appeals and the District of Columbia Superior Court.

# CONTACT US

1775 I Street, NW Suite 1150
Washington, DC 20006

202-505-5309

sjsmith@thesjslawfirm.com

www.TheSJSLawFirm.com

https://twitter.com/TheSJSLawFirm

https://www.facebook.com/
yoursmallbusinessgeneralcounsel

https://www.instagram.com/shavonjsmith